BATTLEFIELDS ACROSS AMERICA

GETTYSBURG

CHRIS HUGHES

Twenty-First Century Books

Brookfield, Connecticut

Twenty-First Century Books
A Division of The Millbrook Press, Inc.
2 Old New Milford Road
Brookfield, Connecticut 06804

5 4 3 2 1

Created and produced in association with Blackbirch Graphics, Inc.

Photo Credits
Cover and pages 6, 8, 11, 14, 18, 24, 26, 40, 45, 47, 48: ©North Wind Picture Archives; pages 32, 37, 52: Library of Congress; page 53: Chris E. Heisey.

All maps by Bob Italiano/©Blackbirch Graphics, Inc.

Library of Congress Cataloging-in-Publication Data
Hughes, Chris.
    Gettysburg / Chris Hughes.
        p.   cm. — (Battlefields across America)
    Includes bibliographical references and index.
    ISBN 0-7613-3012-7 (iib. bdg)
    1. Gettysburg (Pa.), Battle of, 1863. 2. Gettysburg National Military Park (Pa.).
I. Title. II. Series.
E475.53.H85   1998
973.7'349—dc21   98-13538
                                                                                    CIP
                                                                                    AC

16.95

CONTENTS

< 6 >

King Cotton

The abolitionists were not the only ones who did not like slavery. There were Northerners who, although far from ready to embrace African Americans as brothers and sisters, thought slavery was bad business. Slavery had existed in all parts of the country at the time of the American Revolution. But the small farms, craftspeople's shops, and eventually, the factories and banks that formed the basis of the northern economy, could not be efficiently worked by slave labor. As the North prospered without slaves, many there began to think that the South was a "backward" place, holding back the rest of the country. Northern workers feared that if they had to compete against slave labor, their own wages would be lower.

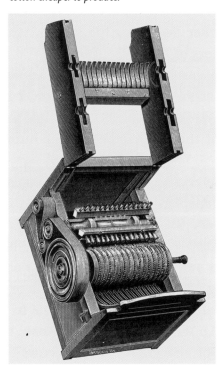

Eli Whitney's invention of the cotton gin made cotton cheaper to produce.

Even in the South, slavery may well have been dying out just after the Revolution. But in 1792 and '93, a man named Eli Whitney invented a device that would make cotton a profitable southern crop. Up until that time, cotton fabric was more expensive than wool, linen, or even silk. It was costly because it took a laborer from 12 to 14 days of work to make a pound of cotton thread. Eli Whitney's device, the cotton gin, increased the amount of fiber that could be cleaned of seeds in an hour by 50 times. Since cotton fiber could be cleaned much more

< 7 >

quickly with the new cotton gin, cotton cloth became cheaper to make and more affordable to buy. As a result, more people could buy cotton cloth. Suddenly cotton became a good cash crop.

The land in what became the states of Tennessee, Georgia, Alabama, and Mississippi was ideal for growing cotton, and large plantations, or farms, became increasingly common. At that time, many people believed that white people could not do heavy labor in the heat of the fields. So slaves—who were thought to be better suited to the climate, since they came from hot Africa—were needed to work the crop. Bringing new slaves from Africa to the United States was outlawed in 1808. Slave owners encouraged their slaves to have many children, who would grow up to work the cotton plantations. Slavery became the basis of the South's economy, and its "peculiar institution." (*Peculiar* in this case did not mean "odd" but "one's own, special.") Southerners thought slavery was necessary for the large-scale farming that to them was a better way of life than the types of businesses many Northerners worked in, such as manufacturing.

The Frontier Becomes a Battleground

While some Americans farmed in the Old South or worked in the factories, businesses, or small farms of the North, others moved westward from 1800 to 1850. They settled lands where Europeans had not lived before. Those who came from the South brought their plantation economy with them. Those from the North brought their small farms. The Northern fears of unfair competition from slave labor grew. Even those who did not particularly care what happened to slaves in the South did not want slavery moving into the newly settled states. Southerners became defensive, and some of them started saying slavery was not just a necessary evil, but a positive

This painting shows two escaped slaves. They are being marched through the streets of Boston to board a ship that would return them to their masters in the South.

good. They were particularly angry about the Underground Railroad "stealing" their "property"—which was what they considered the slaves.

In 1850, Congress passed the Fugitive Slave Law. It greatly helped slave owners trying to recapture escaped slaves in the North. It was this law that Theodore Parker was so proud of having broken. The sight of African Americans being hauled back South by the slave catchers convinced some Northerners to become abolitionists.

States' Rights Becomes an Issue

Other issues increased the rising tension between the North and South. There had long been a question about what the Constitution intended the powers of the states and the federal government to be. As Southerners came to fear that the North wanted to completely

< 9 >

abolish slavery, they argued that a state had the power to ignore a federal law that the state thought was unjust. And since the states had existed before the federal government did, some Southerners thought a state or a group of states could legally secede from, or leave, the Union.

These ideas, which came to be known as "states' rights," were not just a matter of political theory to many Southerners. At the time of the Civil War, Southerners felt strongly about whatever state they lived in. This loyalty was especially deep if a person's family had lived there for a long time. State loyalty was not as evident in the North, where people moved about more and there were more immigrants. Increasingly, Northerners and Southerners felt that they lived in different countries.

Disagreements over slavery, states' rights, and the question of whether farming offered a better way of life than manufacturing all contributed to the widening gap between North and South. People disagreed about all of these issues. Many in the North continued to think that blacks were inferior. Others disliked slavery, but thought the government had no right to ban it. Some abolitionists said if the government didn't outlaw slavery, "freedom-loving" states should leave the Union. In the South, there were those who opposed slavery on economic grounds. But most Southerners came to agree that if the North did not stop trying to interfere with their "peculiar institution," the southern states should secede from the Union.

Lincoln's Election Is the Last Straw

Abraham Lincoln, the Republican candidate for president in 1860, was one of those who personally opposed slavery. He did not think the government had the power to outlaw it completely, but he wanted

< 10 >

it excluded from newly settled land in the West. Southerners feared that Lincoln and his fellow Republicans would succeed in ending slavery altogether. After Lincoln was elected, the Southern states, beginning with South Carolina, made good their threat and seceded from the Union. They formed their own government—the Confederate States of America—and elected Jefferson Davis as their president.

Unfortunately for the South, the one thing most Northerners agreed on by this time was the need to preserve the Union. Lincoln himself was convinced that he had "the legal power, right and duty...to execute the laws and maintain the existing government."[2] Among other things, that meant collecting customs duties (taxes) and defending federal forts in the states that had seceded. In his inaugural address, on March 4, 1861, Lincoln promised to do this, while assuring the South yet again that he would not interfere with slavery where it already existed.

One of the federal forts in a seceded state was Fort Sumter, in the harbor of Charleston, South Carolina. Supplies there were running low, and there was much discussion between Lincoln and his advisors over what should be done. On April 6 the president told the Confederate government of Charleston that he was sending food only—not more arms or soldiers—to the fort. If the South did not interfere, no more troops or arms would be sent there. Instead, the Confederacy decided to attack the fort even before the supplies arrived. On April 12, 1861, Confederate troops fired on Fort Sumter. The Civil War had begun.

Few people expected the war to last very long. Northerners thought the South would give up its claims of independence, while many Southerners assumed the North would eventually lose interest and stop trying to force them back into the Union. As time passed, however, these hopes started to fade away. Throughout the long year

The battle of Antietam lasted only a day, but it was the bloodiest day in American history.

of 1862, both sides began to realize that there was no end in sight to this dreadful war.

The Confederacy seemed to win more often than it lost. Its victories included the first and second battles of Bull Run, in Virginia. Most of the fighting took place in southern lands. The first time Confederate General Robert E. Lee tried to invade the North—on September 17, 1862—he was turned back at the battle of Antietam, in Maryland. It was the bloodiest single day in America's history. As the war continued, casualties on both sides mounted. More and more young men joined the armies and came home wounded, or else died in battle.

GETTYSBURG:
THE ACCIDENTAL BATTLE

In May 1863, things were looking up for the Confederacy in the East. General Robert E. Lee's Army of Northern Virginia had held the field at two large battles in Fredericksburg and Chancellorsville, both in Virginia. But matters were quite different on the western front, where Union General Ulysses S. Grant was closing in on Vicksburg, Mississippi.

Lee proposed to carry the war to the North, marching into Pennsylvania. There, he could get supplies for his troops from the rich farms in the region. He could also threaten the federal capital from its rear and possibly cause Grant to be called away from Vicksburg to defend Washington. At which point, Lee might even be able to take Washington itself. After much discussion and debate, members of the Confederate government accepted Lee's proposal and ordered him to carry it out.

Lee had lost many of his soldiers at Chancellorsville; among the dead was General Stonewall Jackson, whose loss he felt greatly. Still, Lee had some 70,000 to 75,000 soldiers under his command. He concentrated his forces at the town of Culpepper, Virginia, and reorganized his army into three corps, led by Generals Richard Ewell, James Longstreet, and A.P. Hill. The corps, each containing three divisions, prepared to march north through the Shenandoah Valley. Then Lee's army would cross the Potomac into Maryland and continue into Pennsylvania. This was how Lee described the battle he foresaw:

> When they [the Union forces] hear where we are, they will make forced marches to interpose their forces between us and Baltimore and Philadelphia. They will come up [from Virginia] broken down with hunger and hard marching....When they come into Pennsylvania, I shall throw an overwhelming force on their advance, crush it,...and by successive repulses and surprises...create a panic and virtually destroy the army.[1]

< 13 >

< 14 >

Laying his hand on a map left him by Stonewall Jackson, Lee touched an area east of the Allegheny Mountains, saying it would probably be the site of the coming battle. Covered by his hand was the town of Gettysburg, Pennsylvania.

Lee Marches North

All through June of 1863, Lee maneuvered his army north, while the Union commander, Major General "Fighting Joe" Hooker, tried to counter his advance. There were several skirmishes, or minor battles, when troops of one side met up with those of the other.

During their march toward Pennsylvania, Lee's men took off their shoes to cross a creek.

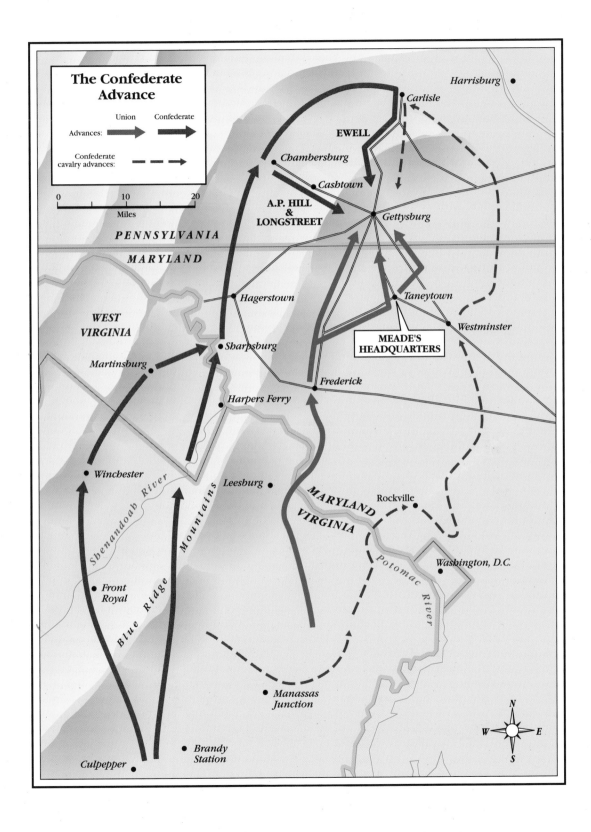

< 16 >

Throughout this period of time, both sides were trying to find out where their opponents were and what they were doing. This kind of investigating is called "reconnaissance." While Hooker was first alerted to the Confederate movements by scouts traveling in hot-air balloons, generally reconnaissance work was the job of the horse soldiers, or cavalry. The cavalry commander doing reconnaissance for Lee was General James Ewell Brown ("Jeb") Stuart. On June 25 he set off to ride around the Union forces. He was going to rejoin Lee farther north. Some unexpected problems kept him out of touch with Lee for several crucial days, however, and by June 27, Lee was desperate for the information Stuart should have been supplying. "Where on earth is my cavalry?"[2] he asked constantly. Because he was out of communication with Stuart—the "eyes and ears" of his army—Lee did not realize how large the Union forces opposing him were.

On the Union side, Hooker was also having a hard time. He wasn't sure how big Lee's forces were, or where they were. And though his

GENERALS AT GETTYSBURG

Confederate

James Archer	James Longstreet
Lewis Armistead	Lafayette McLaws
Jubal Early	William Pender
Richard S. Ewell	James Pettigrew
Henry Heth	George E. Pickett
A.P. Hill	Robert E. Rodes
John Bell Hood	James Ewell Brown
Evander Law	"Jeb" Stuart
Robert E. Lee	Isaac Trimble

Union

John Buford	Henry Hunt
George Armstrong Custer	George G. Meade
Abner Doubleday	John F. Reynolds
John Gibbon	Daniel Sickles
Winfield Scott Hancock	Gouverneur Warren
Oliver Howard	

(This chart lists only some of the generals present at Gettysburg.)

< 17 >

orders were to "fret," or annoy, Lee, he was himself being "fretted" by President Lincoln and General Henry W. Halleck, the Union supreme commander. Halleck vetoed his suggestions for a battle plan and made others that Hooker didn't think appropriate. When Halleck refused to withdraw almost 10,000 men from Harpers Ferry and transfer them to Hooker's command, Hooker ran out of patience. On June 27, he wired Halleck that he could not carry out his instructions with the number of troops at his disposal and asked to be relieved of command. Lincoln and Halleck took Hooker at his word, and General George G. Meade, commanding Hooker's Fifth Corps, was appointed to succeed him. Halleck promised Meade the independence and the Harpers Ferry troops he had refused Hooker. Meade immediately made some promotions and rearranged his line of command.

The Union Advances to Gettysburg

Two events on June 30 helped set the stage for the battle everyone knew was coming. In the afternoon, General John Buford, a Union cavalry commander, rode into Gettysburg. He immediately saw that the town was strategically important. Gettysburg was at the intersection of several roads and had high spots that would make good defense posts. Buford put guards out on the roads and on the heights. His men were armed with a new weapon, the Spencer carbine, which was loaded from the back. It could be loaded and it fired more quickly than the Confederates' muzzle-loading guns. Buford was sure that Lee's army was somewhere near and would attack soon. He told one of his officers, "They will attack you in the morning and they will come booming—skirmishers three-deep. You will have to fight like the devil until supports arrive."[3] To make sure those supports did arrive, Buford requested them from General John F. Reynolds, who commanded the First Corps.

< 18 >

The Confederates Hunt for Shoes

Meanwhile, Lee had finally learned of the Union advance and Meade's promotion from a secret agent. Lee had known Meade when they served in the U.S. Army, and respected him. "General Meade will commit no blunder on my front, and if I make one he will make haste to take advantage of it,"[4] he told his officers. Now he ordered his troops to come together at Cashtown, Pennsylvania, 9 miles west of Gettysburg. On the way, one of General A.P. Hill's division commanders, General Henry Heth, heard that there was a supply of shoes in a nearby town. The Confederates were always short of shoes—they wore them out on the frequent long marches the men undertook, and had few opportunities to replace them. A Union scout, describing Confederate troops in York, Pennsylvania, wrote:

George G. Meade

Their dress was a wretched mixture of all cuts and colors. There was not the slightest attempt at uniformity in this respect. Every man seemed to have put on whatever he could get hold of, without regard to shape or color.... Their shoes, as a general thing, were poor; some of the men were entirely barefooted.[5]

< 19 >

When Heth told Hill about the shoes and requested permission to go get them the next day, Hill agreed. He was sure that the only Union forces there would be some cavalry, "probably a detachment of observation [scouts]."[6] The town where the shoe supply was supposedly located was Gettysburg. (As it turned out, there was no such supply.)

On the evening of June 30, Lee's troops were encamped under rainy skies along the Chambersburg to Baltimore Pike (modern Route 30 follows much of its route). Meade had established his headquarters in Taneytown, Maryland. He decided to take a defensive position, in which he could protect Washington and Baltimore and "hold this army pretty nearly in the position it now occupies until the plans of the enemy" were better known.[7]

Day 1: July 1, 1863

Heth's men left for Gettysburg shortly after dawn. They expected to face a local militia—a small, poorly armed troop made up of men from the town. Instead, they found themselves confronted by two brigades of the Union army. Buford's cavalry had dismounted and in the dark of night dug themselves into good defensive positions behind trees and fences and in ditches. Heth's division numbered over 7,000 men, compared to the 2,700 men in Buford's two brigades. In addition, since Buford's men were cavalry, one out of every four soldiers had to hold the horses and could not fight. Despite the great advantage in numbers held by the Confederates, the Union forces' new Spencer carbines, and the well-organized defense planned by Buford strengthened the Union side.

The Union forces held off the Confederates, giving ground very slowly, and making Heth's men fight for every foot of land they gained. Buford had chosen his spot very well; his soldiers could fall

< 20 >

back from their first positions to higher ground called McPherson's Ridge. From there, they could still protect the highest ground, south of the town. There, two more ridges called Seminary Ridge and Cemetery Ridge ran north to south. As Union soldiers fought to hold their ground, Buford sent desperate calls for help to Reynolds.

Buford directed his men from a tower at the Lutheran Seminary, just west of town. From there he could see his troops battle against the overwhelming numbers of Confederates. Although they fought well for almost two hours, it was clear that they would not be able to hold out much longer. Finally, around 10:00 A.M., just as Buford was starting to fear that his men would have to retreat completely, Reynolds arrived. He had ridden ahead of his corps in response to Buford's messages, and told Buford to hold on a little longer until reinforcements arrived. Reynolds also sent a message back to General Meade at Taneytown, Maryland, about 12 miles south: "The enemy is advancing in strong force. I will fight him inch by inch, and if driven into the town I will barricade the streets and hold him back as long as possible."[8]

The Iron Brigade to the Rescue

Reynolds then rode back to urge his men to come quickly. One of the first units to arrive at McPherson's Ridge was the "Iron" Brigade. The only brigade in the Army of the Potomac made up of regiments from western states, its nickname reflected the brigade's reputation as a very brave and heroic group of soldiers. When the Iron Brigade arrived, the Confederates recognized their distinctive black hats. One soldier shouted, "Thar come the black hats! 'Taint no militia! It's the Army of the Potomac!"[9]

A fierce battle soon began between the brigade and Confederates from Tennessee and Alabama led by General James Archer. One young member of the Iron Brigade described the conflict:

< 21 >

For seven or eight minutes ensued probably the most desperate fight ever waged between artillery and infantry at close range without a particle of cover on either side, bullets hissing, humming and whistling everywhere; cannon roaring; all crash on crash and peal on peal, smoke, dust, splinters, blood, wreck and carnage indescribable.[10]

Although the Iron Brigade forced the Confederates back, they paid a horrible price: 65 percent of their men were lost that day. The Union also lost one of its best generals. Reynolds was shot behind his right ear, and died immediately. Control of the battle fell to General Abner Doubleday, who later turned command over to General Oliver Howard. Archer's command had been destroyed by the Iron Brigade, and Archer himself was captured.

By 11:00 that morning, the battlefield was quiet again while the two armies counted their losses and got ready for the next stage. Since neither Lee nor Meade had planned for this battle to take place, the individual corps and brigade commanders were not sure how strong their attacks should be. Although they had been temporarily stopped, the Confederates were still convinced that they held the advantage of greater numbers. A.P. Hill promised to support Heth's tired men with the division commanded by General William Pender. Hill had also sent word that morning to General Richard S. Ewell, who commanded the Second Corps. Ewell had made the good decision to send two of his own divisions toward Gettysburg. Just before 1:00 P.M., Union General Howard heard that a large Confederate force was approaching the Union's far right side from the north. One of Ewell's divisions, led by General Robert E. Rodes, had arrived.

Ewell had orders from Lee not to stage a major attack until the entire Army of Northern Virginia was united and ready, and he had

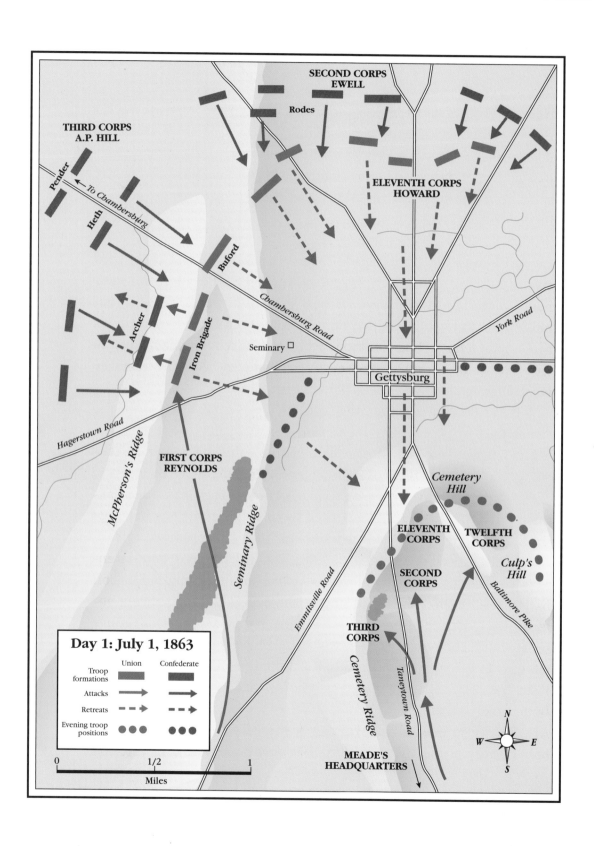

**THIRD CORPS
A.P. HILL**

Pender

← To Chambersburg

Heth

Buford

Chambersburg Road

Archer

Iron Brigade

Seminary □

Hagerstown Road

McPherson's Ridge

**FIRST CORPS
REYNOLDS**

Seminary Ridge

**SECOND CORPS
EWELL**

Rodes

**ELEVENTH CORPS
HOWARD**

York Road

Gettysburg

*Cemetery
Hill*

**ELEVENTH
CORPS**

**TWELFTH
CORPS**

**SECOND
CORPS**

*Culp's
Hill*

Emmitsville Road

**THIRD
CORPS**

Cemetery Ridge

Taneytown Road

Baltimore Pike

Day 1: July 1, 1863

	Union	Confederate
Troop formations		
Attacks	→	→
Retreats	⇢	⇢
Evening troop positions	●●●	●●●

0   1/2   1

Miles

**MEADE'S
HEADQUARTERS**

N
W ✦ E
S

< 23 >

passed those orders on to Rodes. But when Rodes arrived, he thought the Federal right flank, or the far right side of the Union as it faced the Confederates, was unprotected. He decided to attack. By the time his attack was organized, however, Buford's cavalry had spotted the threat and brought word to Howard, who sent his own Eleventh Corps to cover the flank.

Rodes attacked just after 2:00 P.M. In the center he had placed two inexperienced brigades, which were led by commanders who stayed in the rear instead of leading the fight. Both brigades suffered horrible casualties as they were struck by a Union brigade hiding behind a stone wall. The Twenty-Third North Carolina was one of the regiments trapped, and every commissioned officer (ranks from lieutenant and higher) except one was either killed or wounded. An officer with the unit, Captain Vines Turner, later described the massacre:

> *Unarmed, unled as a brigade, we went to our doom. Deep and long must the desolate homes and orphan children of North Carolina rue* [regret] *the rashness of that hour....Unable to advance, unwilling to retreat, the brigade lay down in this hollow and fought the best it could.*[11]

Rodes ordered two more of his brigades to attack next. Eventually, the Confederates' greater numbers started to force the Union back. The Federal line was now almost at a right angle to the Confederates. On the left was the First Corps, facing the remains of Archer's brigade on McPherson Ridge. On the right was the Eleventh Corps, which was held in place by a brigade in Rodes' division.

Lee Makes a Fateful Decision

At about this moment, a new figure arrived at the Confederate line behind McPherson Ridge. Riding his gray horse, Traveler, General

Robert E. Lee arrived at Gettysburg on the first day of fighting there.

Lee had followed the sounds of the guns to the battle. It was not a conflict he had planned or even wanted yet, but Heth's search for shoes and Buford's decision to hold the high ground had transformed what should have been a minor skirmish into a major battle of the Civil War.

Still, Lee was unwilling to commit more forces to the fight, despite the requests of both Hill and Heth. Lee wanted to wait until General James Longstreet's corps arrived to join in the fight, and they were still several hours away. As Lee watched Rodes' men fighting to the east, though, he saw a new cloud of dust. General Jubal Early's division of Ewell's Second Corps was marching to the attack, hoping to close in on the Union's right flank, which was fighting against Rodes. Realizing the opportunity this provided the

< 25 >

Confederacy, Lee ordered Heth and Pender to attack the Federal army's left side.

While Lee watched the battle in its afternoon phase, Meade was still in Taneytown. From there, he ordered one of the Union's most respected generals, Winfield Scott Hancock, to go to Gettysburg and take charge of the conflict. Hancock was not the highest-ranking officer available. Both General Howard and General Daniel Sickles were his superiors. But Meade knew that Hancock had excellent judgment, and he was well respected and trusted by the soldiers.

At Gettysburg, the new Confederate forces meant disaster for the tired Union soldiers. On the Federal right, the Eleventh Corps was the first to break in the face of Early's troops. They pulled back from the fields north of Gettysburg and came through the town on their way to Cemetery Hill, where Howard had left a division and artillery in reserve. Eventually, the Federal left was also forced back to Cemetery Hill. During the fighting, Confederate General Heth was shot in the head. He was badly hurt, but his life was saved by a roll of paper he had stuffed in his hat. His command was taken over by General James Pettigrew.

By late afternoon, the two Union corps were met at Cemetery Hill by General Hancock, who had just arrived from Taneytown. Meade's orders gave Hancock command of the field. This made him the fifth Union general to command the forces at Gettysburg in less than nine hours! Howard resented being replaced by a man who should have served under him, but he could not argue with Meade's direct order. Hancock approved of the location Howard had selected. Cemetery Hill was a good place to make a stand and could be well defended. Still, Hancock knew his forces were badly outnumbered by the Confederates, and it would take all available soldiers to hold off another attack. He ordered the Iron Brigade to occupy nearby Culp's Hill. General Doubleday protested this move, since

Two of the most talented Union commanders at Gettysburg were John Buford and Winfield Scott Hancock. **Brigadier General Buford** was the cavalry leader who first recognized the military value of the hills and ridges of Gettysburg. It is hard to imagine a better defensive location, and much of the credit for the Union victory goes to Buford's selection of Gettysburg as a possible battlefield. Holding his position against overwhelming numbers of Confederates, Buford established himself as a true hero of the war. Four months after the battle of Gettysburg, Buford became fatally ill with typhoid. Before he died, he was promoted to major general for his services rendered at Gettysburg.

John Buford

Winfield Scott Hancock

Like many commanders in both the Union and Confederate armies, **Major General Winfield Scott Hancock** served in the Mexican War. Later, he was assigned to the California Territory, where he became close friends with Lewis Armistead before Armistead left to join the Confederacy. Called "Hancock the Superb," he was an inspiration to his men at Gettysburg. He showed no fear and always seemed to be in the middle of the fight. Hancock recovered from the leg wound he received during Pickett's charge, and went on to a successful post-war life. In 1880, he ran for president of the United States, but was narrowly defeated. He died six years later.

< 27 >

the Iron Brigade was so battered and exhausted, but Hancock would not have his orders questioned. He roared at Doubleday: "Sir, I am in command of this field. Send every man you have!"[12]

The Union was not seriously attacked again that day. Hancock had called for reinforcements, and the Twelfth Corps arrived about 6:00 that evening, soon followed by the Third Corps and, still later that evening, the Second Corps.

In the Confederate camp, Lee had watched his men push the Yankees to Cemetery Hill. He hoped that one final attack might conquer them completely. Lee sent Ewell a message asking him to take Cemetery Hill if Ewell thought the move reasonable. Ewell, who was used to receiving orders, rather than suggestions, chose not to make the attack.

The rebels had clearly won the first day's engagement. They had pushed the Union forces back on all fronts, captured the town of Gettysburg, and inflicted a lot of damage on the two Federal corps they faced. Their failure to make that final attack on Cemetery Hill, however, was costly. The Union army was allowed to hold high, easily defended ground, while the Confederates brought up the rest of the Army of the Potomac. The rebels had also lost a lot of troops—6,500—though not as many as the Union, which lost 9,000.

Day 2: July 2, 1863

The fires in both camps burned long into the night. Sometime after midnight, General Meade and his staff arrived at Cemetery Hill. He had already ordered the remainder of the Army of the Potomac to join with the soldiers at Gettysburg. Seeing the strength of their position and the determination of his troops, he chose to concentrate his entire force in an effort to break the Army of Northern Virginia at Gettysburg.

< 28 >

Less than two miles away, Lee was meeting with his generals too. While the Union leaders were united in their decision to make a stand at Gettysburg, the Confederates were not. Longstreet was the one most strongly opposed to the idea of fighting the next day. He saw that the Federal forces were being reinforced and holding good ground. He knew that Meade would be spending the night preparing for an attack and that the Confederates, who would be fighting uphill, could not expect to surprise or outnumber their enemies.

Longstreet wanted to withdraw from the field and turn the army south toward Washington. By doing this, they could surprise Meade. Since Meade was so new to command, it would probably take him longer than someone more experienced to move his army. Then Meade would have to chase Lee to whatever place Lee chose for the fight. This could guarantee the Confederacy their choice of ground. Although Longstreet had become Lee's most trusted general since Stonewall Jackson's death, Lee did not accept Longstreet's advice at Gettysburg.

Lee was afraid that his soldiers would lose their fighting spirit if he withdrew after winning the battle the day before. He was also limited by the fact that his cavalry leader, Jeb Stuart, had still not been heard from. Without the cavalry, Lee had no way of knowing exactly how large the Union force was or how far it extended. Lee thought that moving his army without that information was too risky. His response to Longstreet was simple, "No, the enemy is there, and I am going to attack him there...they are in position and I am going to whip them or they are going to whip me."[13]

In the Union camp, Meade created a plan. Along the high ground of the ridges and hills, he placed his army into a shape resembling a fishhook. The hooked part rounded Cemetery Hill and Culp's Hill on the Federal right, while to the left, the troops formed

< 29 >

a straight line extending along Cemetery Ridge to a hill called Little Round Top. This formation allowed the Union to keep their reserves in the center, from where they could reach almost any point along the line. By the time all his units had arrived, Meade's force numbered almost 95,000 men, compared to Lee's 75,000.

Lee Orders His Attack

Lee's scouts had mistakenly told him that the Federal line did not extend as far as Little Round Top or its southern neighbor, Big Round Top. He therefore ordered Longstreet's corps to march as quietly as possible toward the Union's left side. From there, Longstreet would attack what Lee assumed was the weak flank, and push on to Cemetery Ridge and Cemetery Hill from the south. In the Confederate center, A.P. Hill was to use two of his divisions to attack Cemetery Hill from the west when Longstreet's corps arrived. To the north, General Ewell's corps was given the order to stage an attack when they heard Longstreet's men begin fighting. Ewell was only supposed to attract some of the Union troops away from Longstreet. He was told to turn the fight into a full-scale attack, however, if he saw an opportunity.

All of these messages were delivered verbally, and many were given to the generals by Lee himself. Usually, battle orders were written out, or at least issued with all the commanders present. In this case, Ewell received his orders apart from Longstreet and Hill, and he never had a written copy. Lee's failure to guarantee that all his generals knew their roles turned out to be costly.

The conflict was to start with Longstreet. His plan was to move his corps southeast as early as possible, but he chose to wait until General Evander Law's brigade joined him around noon. Longstreet's entire corps was now united, except for one division led by

< 30 >

General George Pickett, which could not arrive until late afternoon. It was 3:30 in the afternoon before Longstreet and Law were ready to attack.

Sickles Ignores His Orders

On the Union side, events were not going according to Meade's plan. Shortly after dawn, he had sent his orders out for the final placement of his troops. One of these orders called for the two regiments from the Twelfth Corps on top of Little Round Top to rejoin their corps at Culp's Hill. The troops now responsible for the extreme left of the Union line was the Third Corps, commanded by General Sickles, who was on Cemetery Ridge. Sickles received word that Little Round Top was left undefended, but he never moved any troops up to cover it.

Instead, Sickles examined his own position. The section of Cemetery Ridge he was to cover was the southernmost and lowest part, and in places it was barely a ridge at all. From his position, Sickles could see a peach orchard half a mile west that was higher ground than the ridge he defended. Sickles feared that if the Confederates took that orchard, they could put artillery in it and fire down into his Third Corps. At about 3:00 P.M., he sent his corps forward to march to the orchard. He placed his center in the peach orchard and across a wheat field and his left flank in a group of boulders called Devil's Den.

Sickles' move (called Sickles' Salient, or "exposed angle") was a dangerous mistake. It isolated his entire corps and exposed the Union's left flank, which now had to be guarded by Hancock's Second Corps. When Meade heard about Sickles' move, he rode out to see it himself. In the face of Meade's anger, Sickles realized his error and offered to move his men back. Just then, guns started firing. It was too late for Sickles to withdraw.

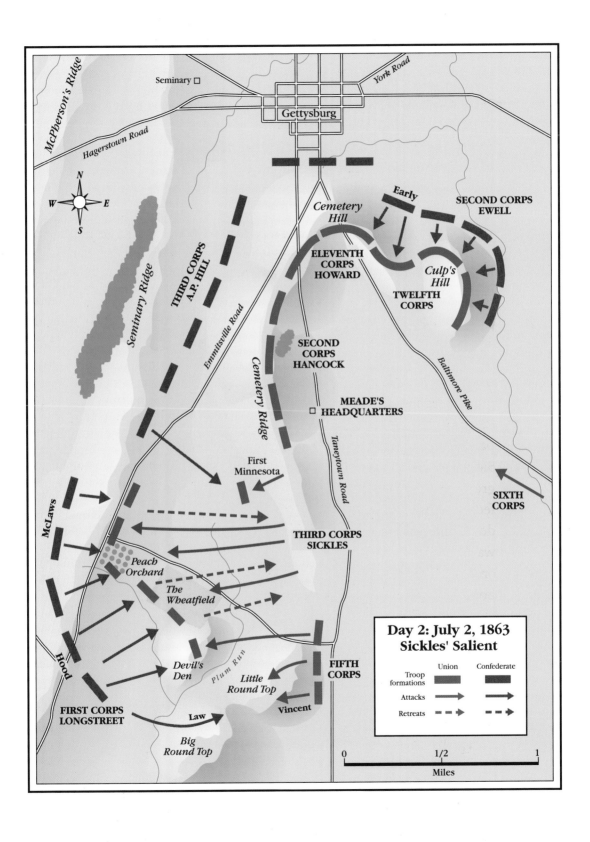

McPherson's Ridge

Seminary □

York Road

Gettysburg

Hagerstown Road

Seminary Ridge

N
W   E
S

THIRD CORPS
A.P. HILL

Emmitsville Road

Cemetery Ridge

Cemetery Hill

Early

SECOND CORPS
EWELL

ELEVENTH CORPS
HOWARD

Culp's Hill

TWELFTH CORPS

SECOND CORPS
HANCOCK

Baltimore Pike

MEADE'S HEADQUARTERS □

First Minnesota

Taneytown Road

SIXTH CORPS

McLaws

THIRD CORPS
SICKLES

Peach Orchard

The Wheatfield

Devil's Den

Plum Run

FIFTH CORPS

Little Round Top

Vincent

FIRST CORPS
LONGSTREET

Law

Big Round Top

Day 2: July 2, 1863
Sickles' Salient

	Union	Confederate
Troop formations		
Attacks		
Retreats		

0   1/2   1

Miles

< 32 >

When Longstreet's corps arrived at the peach orchard, they expected to find that area free of Union soldiers. Instead, they found the Third Corps hidden in the trees. Although Longstreet's two division commanders, Lafayette McLaws and John Bell Hood, both urged him to change the plan of battle, Longstreet refused. He was going to follow Lee's commands and attack the Union's left flank, even though the enemy was not where Lee had told him to

This drawing of Longstreet's men attacking the left side of the Union army was published in Harpers Weekly *magazine.*

< 33 >

expect it. Both McLaws and Hood strongly protested the plan, but Longstreet ordered them ahead.

Longstreet's 20,000 veterans attacked Sickles' 10,000 men in a furious battle that lasted hours. Sickles himself lost a leg in the fight, and his men were eventually pushed out of the orchard and back to Cemetery Ridge. While McLaws' men focused on the orchard and the wheat field, Hood's men circled south to attack Devil's Den and the Round Tops. After fierce fighting at the base of Big Round Top, Colonel William Oates led the Fifteenth Alabama to the peak of Big Round Top, which was the highest point for miles—305 feet above the surrounding plain. From his vantage point, Oates could see the entire Federal line, all the way to Cemetery Hill and Culp's Hill. From here he could fire cannons along the undefended side of the Federals; they would have no defense. But Big Round Top was too steep and wooded to bring artillery to the top. Nearby Little Round Top, however, which appeared undefended, could be used for that same purpose.

Heroism at Little Round Top

Colonel Oates was not the only officer to realize the importance of the Round Tops for both sides. Fortunately for the Union, their chief engineer, General Gouverneur Warren, had also seen the danger of the undefended Little Round Top. Colonel Strong Vincent agreed to defend the hill with his brigade from the Fifth Corps. He rushed his men up the slope, placing the Twentieth Maine on the far left. This position represented the extreme left of the entire Army of the Potomac, and Vincent told the men to hold their place "at all hazards." As one Union private remembered:

It was a critical moment. If that line was permitted to turn the Federal flank, Little Round Top was untenable [impossible to hold],

< 34 >

and with this little mountain in the Confederate's possession, the whole position would be untenable. It was a most fortunate fact for the Union cause that in command of the Twentieth Maine was Colonel Joshua Lawrence Chamberlain.[14]

As Oates received the order to take Little Round Top, Vincent's forces were getting into position. By the time the Confederates arrived, the Union was ready. Instead of finding the almost empty hill Oates had seen, his men now ran headlong into Vincent's brigade. The fighting was the worst on the far left, where the Confederates hoped to hit the Union forces from the side.

The 386 men of the Twentieth Maine were pushed from their position five times, but each time they fought their way back. Finally, after more than an hour, the Maine men were almost out of ammunition. Knowing that one more strong Confederate charge could break his line, Chamberlain was forced into a decision: retreat or attack? He drew his sword and ordered his men to fix their bayonets to their guns. While he yelled "charge," every man in the regiment who could still run raced down the hill at the amazed Confederates. The Union's approach was so ferocious, many of the Confederates surrendered without a fight. Chamberlain's men took about 90 prisoners and held Little Round Top for the Union, but they had lost over one third of their regiment in the fight. Chamberlain was later awarded the Congressional Medal of Honor for his brave defense.

To the west, the Union was in desperate trouble. Sickles' isolated troops in the peach orchard, wheat field, and Devil's Den were being driven back by the Confederates. Some of the most severe clashes came in the area of scattered boulders called Devil's Den. A private from Massachusetts remembered the sound of the clash years later:

< 35 >

The hoarse and indistinguishable orders of commanding officers, the screaming and bursting of shells, canister and shrapnel as they tore through the struggling masses of humanity, the death screams of wounded animals, the groans of their human companions, wounded and dying and trampled underfoot by hurrying batteries, riderless horses and the moving lines of battle...a perfect hell on earth, never, perhaps to be equaled, certainly not to be surpassed, nor ever to be forgotten in a man's lifetime. It has never been effaced from my memory, day or night, for fifty years.[15]

In the massed confusion, there were many opportunities for heroism on both sides. Perhaps the finest story of bravery is that of the First Minnesota. The fight for the Devil's Den and the peach orchard had left a gap in the Union lines along Cemetery Ridge, and A.P. Hill had sent a brigade to make the attack. Seeing the danger, General Hancock realized he needed to stall the Confederates in order to gain time to get reinforcements to the gap. The closest regiment was the 262-man First Minnesota. He ordered them to charge the 1700-man Confederate brigade. As one survivor stated, "Every man realized in an instant what that order meant—death or wounds to us all, the sacrifice of a regiment to gain a few minutes' time and save the position."[16] The tiny regiment fixed their bayonets and charged the shocked brigade, pushing them back. The cost of the successful charge was high; only 47 men of that regiment survived unhurt, making the 82 percent of their comrades who fell the highest percentage of casualties taken by any Union regiment in the war. In describing the attack, General Hancock said, "There is no more gallant deed recorded in history."[17]

Eventually, the western side of the Union line was pushed back from Sickles' Salient. But they held Meade's intended positions: from Little Round Top north along Cemetery Ridge to Cemetery Hill.

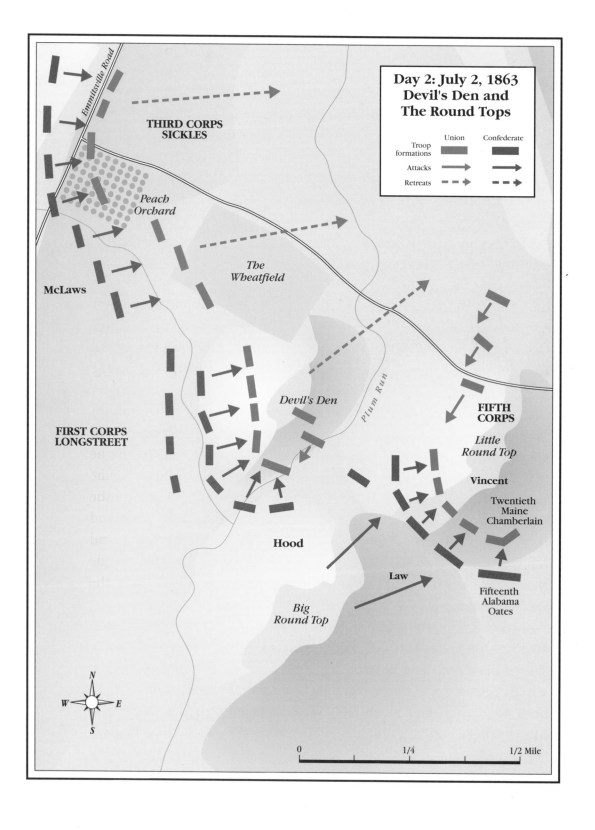

Day 2: July 2, 1863
Devil's Den and
The Round Tops

Troop formations — Union / Confederate
Attacks
Retreats

Emmitsville Road

THIRD CORPS
SICKLES

Peach
Orchard

McLaws

The
Wheatfield

Devil's Den

Plum Run

FIFTH
CORPS

Little
Round Top

Vincent

Twentieth
Maine
Chamberlain

FIRST CORPS
LONGSTREET

Hood

Law

Big
Round Top

Fifteenth
Alabama
Oates

N
W   E
S

0   1/4   1/2 Mile

This Confederate soldier was killed in the fierce fighting at Little Round Top.

Sickles' exposed position cost the Union a great many soldiers, but some historians think it might have saved the battle. They argue that by forcing the Confederates to fight their way through the peach orchard and Devil's Den, Sickles broke the strength of the rebels' attack. By the time they reached the Round Tops and Cemetery Ridge, the Confederates were too badly scattered and weakened to take the Union's left flank as Lee wanted. Others argue that if Sickles had obeyed Meade's orders, he could have held the Union flank with a much lower loss of life.

Ewell Fails to Follow the Plan

To the north, Lee's plan never went into effect. General Ewell was supposed to attack the Federal right when Longstreet's attack began on the left. For some reason, when Longstreet's attack finally began in the afternoon, Ewell did not hear the guns until the fighting was

< 38 >

well under way. Then, rather than ordering his soldiers to attack, he ordered his artillery to begin firing.

Ewell's men fired at the Federal positions for more than two hours, while the Union cannons shot back. Since the Union had spent the day digging into their positions, the Confederate shells did little damage. Instead, the Northern gunners slowly destroyed their Southern counterparts. When Ewell finally did order the attack, it was after 6:30 in the evening. His men pushed forward and took the lower edges of Culp's Hill before they were stopped.

That ended the fighting for the day. The Confederates had pushed the Union forces back from the peach orchard and had taken some territory at the foot of Culp's Hill, but they had failed to make any important gains on the high ground still held by Meade. Each side had lost some 9,000 casualties in the day's fighting, and both sides knew the battle was far from over. Meade guessed that since Lee's attempts on the flanks had failed, he would probably try to hit the Union center the next day.

At Lee's headquarters, Jeb Stuart had finally appeared about noon. He had captured 125 wagons and teams from the North, but he had been absent when Lee needed him the most; to scout the Federal position and keep Lee informed of its location. Now, Lee had to control his anger and plan for the next day. As Meade had correctly guessed, he hoped to crush the North with one devastating blow at the center of their line.

Day 3: July 3, 1863

In his camp, General Lee weighed his options. His failure to push the Federals from their strongest defensive posts did not convince Lee to abandon his hope for victory. Longstreet again argued for withdrawing and forcing Meade to follow them south, but Lee refused to

< 39 >

leave this field of battle. Originally, Lee's plan for that third day was for Longstreet to attack the Federal left while Ewell hit the right and stormed Culp's Hill. In the meantime, Stuart was to go behind the Union and harass its messengers in order to disrupt Federal communications.

At daylight, however, the Union Twelfth Corps was given the order to take back their trenches on Culp's Hill. After several bloody hours, Ewell's forces were pushed back from the hill, and by 11:00 in the morning, they had withdrawn. At the same time, Longstreet was trying to find a way to force the Union to pull their lines closer together by attacking them on their far left side. Without Ewell's help on the right, that plan was impossible, however. Lee then put together what he hoped would be his master stroke.

General Pickett was one of the most talented young leaders in the Confederate Army. His appointment to West Point had been secured by Abraham Lincoln, but like so many Confederate officers, he resigned from the army to join the Confederacy and defend his home state of Virginia. Pickett arrived at Gettysburg on July 2, anxious to join the battle. He was upset that his men had missed the fighting on that day, and Lee promised to give them a chance on July 3. Ordering Longstreet to make the arrangements, Lee wanted Pickett to lead his division in an attack against the center of the Federal line. This would mean marching just over 12,000 men almost three-quarters of a mile across open fields in plain view of the Federal guns.

Longstreet was closer to refusing an order than he had ever been before. "General Lee," he said, "I have been a soldier all my life. I have been with soldiers engaged in fights by couples, by squads, companies, regiments, divisions, and armies, and should know as well as anyone what soldiers can do. It is my opinion that no fifteen thousand men ever arrayed for battle can take that position."[18] Unconvinced, Lee ordered Longstreet to make the arrangements.

< 40 >

The Artillery Duel

The contest would begin with the Confederate artillery blasting away at the Union guns in order to destroy them. Once word was given, the men would start their march, aiming for a small clump of oak trees on the crest of Cemetery Ridge. The trees were near a bend in a stone fence called the Angle. James Pettigrew and Isaac Trimble would lead the other divisions with Pickett. Pettigrew was taking the place of the wounded Harry Heth, and Trimble was leading two brigades from what was left of Pender's division. These were men he had never led or even met before.

Some Confederate soldiers wait for the end of the artillery duel, which preceded Pickett's charge.

Colonel Edward Porter Alexander was the artillery officer given command of the initial artillery attack. Just before noon, he received a note from Longstreet, who was still resisting Lee's plan. Longstreet told Alexander to judge whether or not his bombardment was successful before he allowed Pickett to attack. Alexander responded that the decision to attack needed to be made before he used his artillery. From his position, once the guns started firing he wouldn't be able to see anything but smoke. The Union lines would be obscured. It had to be Longstreet's decision.

With regret, General Longstreet ordered the artillery to begin firing at 1:00 P.M. As he later wrote, "With my knowledge of the situation, I could see the desperate and hopeless nature of the charge and the cruel slaughter it would cause."[19] Alexander's 170 guns fired for nearly two hours against 80 Union guns. Slowly, the Union artillery fell silent, and through the smoke, Alexander watched them withdraw from the Angle. Alexander realized that his own ammunition was running low, and he assumed that he had outlasted the Union's supply of ammunition. In spite of his earlier refusal to give the order, Alexander sent a note to Pickett telling him that if he was going to attack, he should do so immediately, while Alexander still had some ammunition to support him.

On the Union side, the sudden shelling at 1:00 P.M. shattered the silence that had surrounded the men since Ewell's withdrawal from Culp's Hill. As the Union men scrambled to get their cannons in position to fire back, Confederate shells damaged Meade's headquarters and the area behind most of the Union troops. The Confederate guns were aimed slightly too high to do as much damage as they might have otherwise, but as one soldier put it, "It seemed that nothing four feet from the ground could live. All we had to do was flatten out a little thinner, and our empty stomachs did not prevent that."[20] Many of the men remembered the bravery of General

< 42 >

Hancock, who stayed calmly on his horse throughout the barrage, calming his men's fears. The Union artillery response had been better aimed: Pickett's division alone suffered 500 casualties as they waited in the trees for the order to advance.

The Union gunners were aware that the Confederate fire was probably the first stage of an attack, and they worked to save their ammunition. After two hours, the order was given to cease firing and remove the damaged cannons from the field. This was designed to convince the Confederates that they had won the artillery duel, while in truth the Union still had enough ammunition to do great damage to an infantry attack. The plan worked, and Alexander sent out his note to Pickett.

Pickett's Charge

When that note came in, the three Confederate divisions began to advance steadily, as described by an aide to Union General John Gibbon:

> More than half a mile their front extends, more than a thousand yards the dull gray masses deploy, man touching man, rank pressing rank, and line supporting line. The red flags wave, their horsemen gallop up and down; the arms of eighteen thousand men, barrel and bayonet, gleam in the sun, a sloping forest of flashing steel. Right on they move as with one soul, in perfect order...magnificent, grim, irresistible.[21]

As the Confederate soldiers marched, the Union cannons renewed their fire with devastating effect. The Confederates had not been as careful to save their ammunition as the Union was, and Alexander had little artillery left to support the charge. There were also Union troops in positions along the side of the march, who attacked the flanks of the Confederates throughout their approach.

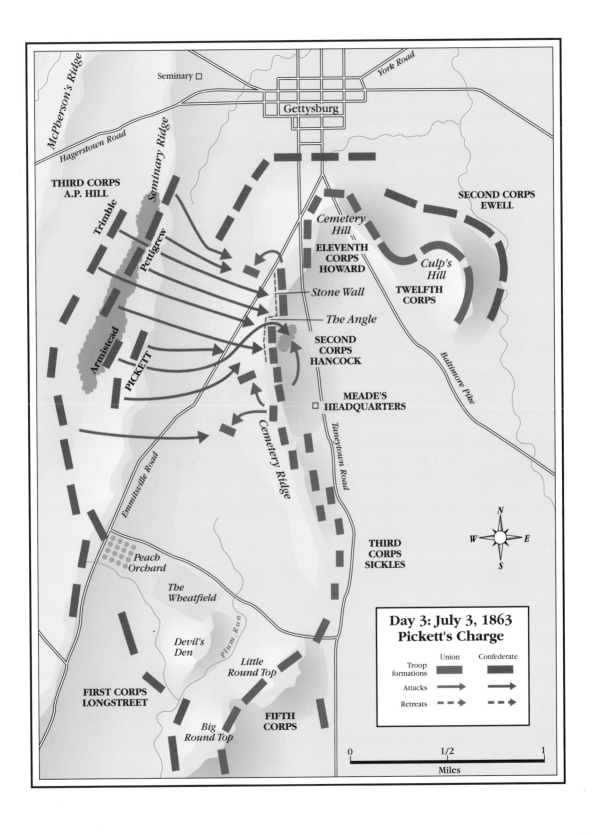

McPherson's Ridge

Seminary □

York Road

Gettysburg

Hagerstown Road

Seminary Ridge

THIRD CORPS
A.P. HILL

Trimble

Pettigrew

Armistead

PICKETT

SECOND CORPS
EWELL

Cemetery
Hill

ELEVENTH
CORPS
HOWARD

Culp's
Hill

TWELFTH
CORPS

Stone Wall

The Angle

SECOND
CORPS
HANCOCK

MEADE'S
□ HEADQUARTERS

Baltimore Pike

Cemetery Ridge

Taneytown Road

THIRD
CORPS
SICKLES

Emmitsville Road

Peach
Orchard

The
Wheatfield

Devil's
Den

Plum Run

Little
Round Top

FIRST CORPS
LONGSTREET

Big
Round Top

FIFTH
CORPS

N
W E
S

Day 3: July 3, 1863
Pickett's Charge

	Union	Confederate
Troop formations		
Attacks		
Retreats		

0   1/2   1

Miles

< 44 >

Still, the Confederates advanced, even in the face of the thousands of rifles that poured deadly fire into their ranks. Despite terrible losses, thousands of the rebels reached the base of Cemetery Ridge and began to charge up the slope, urged on by officers like the young lieutenant who waved his sword, shouting, "Home, boys, home! Remember, home is over beyond those hills!"[22]

As the remaining Confederate forces drew closer to the Angle and the crest of the hill, their situation became even worse. Regiments of Federals hidden behind stone walls rose up in their faces and delivered crushing volleys of rifle fire. Finally, a section of Pickett's division reached the stone wall at the Angle and stormed over the top. They were led by General Lewis Armistead, with his cap on top of his sword, urging his men to go far inside the Union lines. Armistead was shot down, but his men continued forward to the copse of trees. There, they were overwhelmed by a charge of Union soldiers. In less than five minutes, every Confederate soldier who had crossed the stone wall was killed, wounded, or captured.

Armistead himself, when found by Union soldiers, sent a greeting to General Hancock. Before the war the two had been great friends, and they had hoped to resume their relationship after the conflict ended. It was not to be. Armistead sent his personal belongings to Hancock so they could be delivered to his family. Armistead died, not knowing that Hancock had also been hit and lay wounded not far away. Hancock survived his wound, but he grieved for his friend who had chosen the other side. Throughout the Civil War, this tragic scene would be repeated. Men on one side of the conflict were often fighting against friends and even relatives on the other side.

With the end of the fight at the Angle, the Confederate forces began to pull back across the fields, under fire the entire time. Close to half the soldiers who made the charge had fallen in the attack.

It would be hard to imagine two more different commanders than Major Generals James Longstreet and James Ewell Brown ("Jeb") Stuart. **Longstreet** was a solid, stubborn man who believed in the value of a defensive war, and tried to argue Lee out of his intended attacks at Gettysburg. Married to Maria Louise Garland and the father of ten children, Longstreet became a businessman after the war. He served as minister to Turkey when his friend, Union General Ulysses S. Grant, became president in 1869. Longstreet lived until 1904, and died at the age of 83.

James Longstreet

Jeb Stuart was a fiery, excitable man, and probably the finest cavalry officer in the Civil War. He loved to challenge himself and his men with daring acts.

James Ewell Brown ("Jeb") Stuart

More than once, he led his cavalry in a full circle around the entire Union army. When he did this in the days prior to the battle at Gettysburg, however, the Confederates paid a high price. Had Stuart done his job and provided Lee with information on the Union army, Lee could have better judged the size and position of Meade's forces. He might even have accepted Longstreet's proposal to withdraw and choose better ground.

When Stuart finally did arrive, he failed in his main military assignment, which was to attack the Union forces from behind while Pickett's charge unfolded. Stuart was killed in battle near the end of the war. He was survived by his wife, Flora, and their two children.

< 46 >

In Pickett's own division, fewer than two men returned for every five who had marched. He had lost all 15 of his regimental commanders and 16 of the 17 field officers below them. In less than one hour, his division was destroyed. Over the same period of time, General Stuart's cavalry had been stopped by a smaller Union force, led by General George Armstrong Custer, among others. (He would later become famous for his unsuccessful stand against the Cheyenne and Sioux Indians at Little Bighorn on June 25, 1876.)

As Picket returned to the Confederate lines, he was approached by General Lee, who feared a Union counterattack. Lee told him, "General Pickett, place your division in the rear of this hill, and be ready to repel the advance of the enemy should they follow up their advantage." With tears in his eyes, Pickett replied, "General Lee, I have no division now." Lee's response was gentle. "Come, General Pickett, this has been my fight, and upon my shoulders rests the blame. The men and officers of your command have written the name of Virginia as high today as it has ever been written before."[23]

As it turned out, Lee did not have to fear a counterattack. Although several of Meade's officers tried to convince him that the Union's advantage offered Meade a chance to destroy the Army of Northern Virginia once and for all, Meade declined. He appeared to be satisfied with having held off the Confederates' attack. Although some historians have blamed Meade for his failure to continue the fight to the end, the fact is that any attack would have meant moving his entire army, and charging across the open plain that had just served to defeat Pickett. In addition, Meade had only been in command of the army for six days, and three of those days had been among the bloodiest of the war. He had lost Reynolds, Sickles, and Hancock, as well as many other important division and brigade leaders. Finally, Meade had no way of knowing exactly how badly Lee's army was hurt, or how low their artillery ammunition had fallen.

Pickett's charge up Cemetery Ridge resulted in massive casualties, just as Longstreet had anticipated.

< 48 >

The Wreck of the Battle Storm

The next day was July 4, 1863. Independence Day carried a new meaning for the Union soldiers on the field. Lee's army withdrew that day and headed back to Virginia. There were various skirmishes after Meade sent his cavalry, and eventually his infantry, in late efforts to catch Lee before he recrossed the Potomac. But with great planning and good fortune, the Army of Northern Virginia made its crossing. It would never again threaten Union soil. Later, the Union men learned that their victory at Gettysburg had been matched by equally good news from the West: General Grant had defeated the Confederates at Vicksburg, on the Mississippi River, and the South's main communication and supply route was cut in two.

On the field, though, the remains of a terrible battle were everywhere to be seen. In a town of 2,400 people, more than ten

Lee's forces retreated from Gettysburg and headed for Virginia. Their invasion of the North had failed.

< 49 >

times that number of dead and wounded soldiers were left after the armies departed. The Confederates had lost close to 28,000 men dead, wounded, or missing, and the Union lost 23,000. Gettysburg was the bloodiest conflict ever to occur on American soil. A New Jersey soldier who volunteered to help bury the dead wrote his impression of the field:

> *Burial parties were sent out, and those who could get away from their commands went out to view the scene of carnage, and surely it was a scene never to be forgotten. Upon the open fields...in crevices of the rocks, behind fences, trees and buildings; in thickets, where they had crept for safety only to die in agony; by stream or wall or hedge, wherever the battle had raged or their wakening steps could carry them, lay the dead.... All around was the wreck the battle storm leaves in its wake.*[24]

That afternoon, a thunderstorm helped wash away the smells and blood of the battle, but no amount of water could ever wash the memory of those three days from the minds of the men who had been at Gettysburg.

Conclusion

Gettysburg was the "high-water mark" of the Confederacy. This was as deep as the Confederate army ever penetrated into Union territory. The battle also marks the beginning of the Army of Northern Virginia's decline. During the remaining 21 months of the Civil War, the army never fully recovered from the massive losses it suffered. The bloodiest battle in America's bloodiest war, Gettysburg is remembered for the heroism of the soldiers who fought there, and the horrible loss of life and talent that are part of any war.

PART THREE
HISTORY REMEMBERED

More than 7,000 men died on the battlefield at Gettysburg, and thousands of the bodies were left on the field when the armies departed. The Union soldiers had worked to bury many of the men in shallow graves near where they had fallen, but these graves were not designed to be permanent.

Most descriptions of the Gettysburg battlefield by reporters, visitors, and photographers who came there in the weeks following the battle focused on the horrible smell of the dead men and horses left rotting in the hot summer sun.

Pennsylvania's governor, Andrew Curtin, decided to solve the problem while also honoring the fallen, by creating a soldiers' cemetery. A 17-acre spot near Cemetery Hill was chosen. On November 19, 1863, the cemetery was dedicated. The main speaker was Edward Everett, who was considered one of the finest public speakers in the nation. As a courtesy, an invitation had also been sent to President Lincoln. To everyone's surprise, the president accepted.

The Gettysburg Address

Lincoln thought this would be an excellent opportunity for him to remind people of the reasons they were fighting the war. After Everett's two hour-speech, Lincoln rose, holding two sheets of paper. In a talk that only lasted a few minutes, Lincoln made history with what has been called the finest short speech ever made in the English language.

It began with a reference to the Declaration of Independence, which calls all men equal. Lincoln then discussed the survival of the nation, and praised the men "who here gave their lives that that nation might live." Finally, he stated that the men who had died had already blessed the burial ground more than he ever could:

< 51 >

The short speech that Lincoln gave at Gettysburg is one of the most famous given by any American president.

The world will little note nor long remember what we say here, but it can never forget what they did here. It is for us, the living, rather to be dedicated here to the unfinished work that they have thus far so nobly carried on...that we highly resolve that the dead shall not have died in vain, that the nation shall, under God, have a new birth of freedom, and that the government of the people, by the people, and for the people, shall not perish from the earth.[1]

Gettysburg National Military Park

Thirty-two years after the dedication of the soldiers' cemetery, Gettysburg National Military Park was established by the federal government. Covering almost 6,000 acres, the park stands as a monument to the largest battle ever waged in the Western Hemisphere and the bloodiest battle of the Civil War.

More than 1,600 plaques and statues scattered throughout the park serve as reminders of the men and locations made famous by that battle. Little Round Top, Devil's Den, the peach orchard, and

< 53 >

the Angle all evoke memories of the men who fought and in many cases died there.

The park includes the Soldiers' National Cemetery, where the bodies of over 7,000 soldiers—more than 3,500 from the Civil War—are buried. This was the site of Lincoln's famous Gettysburg Address. A copy of it is often displayed there during the summer, on loan from the Library of Congress. The cemetery was open for burial to all U.S. veterans until 1972, when the cemetery ran out of space.

Location and Address Gettysburg National Military Park is off Route 15, one mile south of Gettysburg, at 97 Taneytown Road, Gettysburg, PA 17325. Telephone: (717) 334-1124.

Operating Hours Daily, 6:00 A.M.–10:00 P.M. for the grounds; 8:00 A.M.–5:00 P.M. for the Visitor Center (open until 6:00 P.M. in the summer). The park is closed Thanksgiving, Christmas Day, and New Year's Day.

Entrance Fees There is no fee to enter the park. The Cyclorama Center and the Electric Map are both $3.00 for adults, $2.50 for seniors, and $1.50 for children (ages 6–16).

Snow covers the field where so many died in the fight for Little Round Top. Now called the "Valley of Death," the field lies within Gettysburg National Military Park.

The Soldiers' National Cemetery was dedicated just months after the battle of Gettysburg.

Exhibits and Special Events   More than 1.5 million people pass through the park every year. The Visitor Center includes the Gettysburg Museum of the Civil War, which has a large collection of guns, uniforms, and ammunition. In the auditorium is the Electric Map, which shows troop movements with colored lights as a narrator describes the battle. There is also a Cyclorama Center. A 360-foot oil painting depicting Pickett's Charge lines the walls of this round building, where a 20-minute sound and light program is presented. A 20-minute film on the battle entitled *Gettysburg, 1863*, is presented in the auditorium at the Cyclorama Center.

The park can be explored on foot, bicycle, horseback, or by car. No full reenactments are permitted on the grounds of the battlefield, but private organizations hold reenactments every summer near the park. (The one exception to the rule against reenactments on the battlefield came in 1992, when 5,000 reenactors joined hundreds of actors and film crew members for the filming of *Gettysburg*. This movie, based on the Pulitzer Prize-winning book, *The Killer Angels*, by Michael Shaara, is considered one of the most realistic wartime films ever made.) In addition, there are living history programs

< 55 >

at the park most spring and summer weekends. These include demonstrations of Civil War cavalry, artillery, and infantry, as well as battlefield medical methods.

Related Points of Interest

The city of Gettysburg has a number of sites connected with the Civil War and the battle of Gettysburg. Many of these are seasonal attractions, open only from the spring through the fall. Most are in town, within walking distance of each other.

"The Conflict" Theater is designed particularly for students and their families. It features several films and live presentations on the battle and related historical events. Among the theatrical productions are a 45-minute stage presentation, called "Lincoln Speaks," which is followed by a question-and-answer session with an actor who plays the role of President Lincoln.

This statue honoring the Fortieth New York Infantry for their valor at Devil's Den is only one of many memorials on the Gettysburg battlefield.

< 56 >

The Confederate States Armory and Museum features Confederate and Union weapons, including small arms and the bayonets that were so important at Little Round Top and other battle sites. On the edge of the battlefield is the National Tower, which provides a 360-degree view of the battlefield along with a sound program. The Gettysburg History Center features a 16,000-piece battlefield diorama, or model, with a sound and light show.

General Lee's Headquarters is where Robert E. Lee and his commanders made their battle plans on the night of July 1. It contains a collection of Civil War relics and items that traveled with General Lee, such as eating utensils, clothing, and the table where he made his battle plans. The Soldier's National Museum was Union General Howard's headquarters during the battle. After the war it became the Soldiers National Orphanage. Now a museum, it contains 60 displays, including military miniatures, weapons, and photographs.

Special Events There are also some special events that are worth attending in Gettysburg, such as the annual Memorial Day parade—one of the oldest in the nation. Since 1867, the parade has included a ceremony at Gettysburg National Cemetery, where children place fresh flowers on the soldiers' graves and guest speakers address the crowd. The last week in June and first week in July are marked by Gettysburg Civil War Heritage Days. This event honors the anniversary of the battle with living history encampments, concerts, lectures, fireworks, and battle reenactments. Heritage Days are accompanied by several related annual events: a Civil War Collectors Show and a Civil War Book Fair. In addition, Gettysburg College holds a Civil War Institute during the first week in July with lectures and tours by prominent scholars. November 19 is marked each year with an observance of the anniversary of Lincoln's Gettysburg Address. Afterwards comes Remembrance Day, on the following Saturday, with a parade of reenactors in Civil War dress and a

< 57 >

wreath-laying ceremony. The ceremony takes place at the Albert Woolson Monument.

Locations, Admission, and Hours

The Civil War Institute, Gettysburg College, North Washington Street, Gettysburg, PA 17325. Telephone: (717) 337-6590.

Confederate States Armory and Museum, 528 Baltimore Street, Gettysburg, PA 17325. Telephone: (717) 337-2340. Please call for hours, which vary by season. Admission is $1.50.

"The Conflict" Theater, 213 Steinwehr Avenue, Gettysburg, PA 17325. Telephone: (717) 334-8002. Open Monday, Tuesday, Thursday and Friday 11:00 A.M.–5:00 P.M.; Saturday 10:00 A.M.–6:00 P.M. and Sunday 1:00–5:00 P.M. Admission is $5.00 for adults and $4.00 for children. Show times vary for "Lincoln Speaks." Admission is $6.00 for adults and $5.00 for children.

Gettysburg History Center, 610 Taneytown Road, Gettysburg, PA 17325. Telephone: (717) 334-1288. Hours vary by season. Admission is $4.50 for adults and $3.50 for children.

General Lee's Headquarters, 401 Buford Avenue, Gettysburg, PA 17325. Telephone: (717) 334-3141. Hours vary by season. Admission is $2.00. Children under age 12 are admitted free.

National Tower, Route 134 (opposite the National Park Visitor Center), Gettysburg, PA 13725. Telephone: (717) 334-6754. Hours vary by season. Admission is $5.00 for adults and $3.00 for children.

Soldiers' National Museum, 777 Baltimore Street, Gettysburg, PA 17325. Telephone: (717) 334-4890. Hours vary by season. Admission is $5.25 for adults and $3.25 for children.

For general tour information and upcoming special events, the best source is the Gettysburg Convention and Visitors Bureau, 35 Carlisle Street, Gettysburg, PA 17325. Telephone: (717) 334-6274.

CHRONOLOGY OF THE CIVIL WAR

November 1860	Abraham Lincoln, Republican, elected president of the United States.
December 1860	South Carolina becomes the first Southern state to secede from the Union.
February 1861	Six Southern states that had seceded form the Confederate States of America.
April 1861	Confederate forces fire on Union Fort Sumter in Charleston, SC, and the Civil War begins.
July 1861	Union forces defeated at the battle of Bull Run in Virginia. First major battle of the war.
April 1862	Battle of Shiloh
September 1862	Union soldiers push back Confederate invasion of Maryland at the battle of Antietam.
December 1862	Union suffers massive casualties at the battle of Fredericksburg, in Virginia.
January 1863	Lincoln issues the Emancipation Proclamation, freeing all slaves in Confederate territories.
May 1863	Confederates decisively defeat Union forces at the battle of Chancellorsville, Virginia.
June 1863	Confederate General Robert E. Lee and Union General "Fighting Joe" Hooker maneuver north through Maryland and Pennsylvania.
July 1–3, 1863	Battle of Gettysburg. Union General George G. Meade, succeeding Hooker just days before the battle, defeats Lee on third day of fighting. Lee escapes to the South in heavy rain. This would be the last Confederate attempt to invade the North.
July 4, 1863	Grant's army captures Vicksburg, Mississippi, completing the Union takeover of the Mississippi River, splitting the Confederacy in two.

< 59 >

March 1864	General Grant appointed head of all Union forces by President Lincoln.
May–July 1864	Grant's army marches into Virginia and begins a series of bloody battles with Lee's forces across the state from north to south.
August 1864– April 1865	Grant and Lee dig in for a long siege of trench warfare south of Petersburg, Virginia. The siege will last 9 months.
September 1864	General William Tecumseh Sherman captures Atlanta, Georgia. Sherman begins his famous "March to the Sea."
late 1864	Sherman marches through Georgia, burning everything in his path, and reaches Savannah on Christmas Day.
January 1865	Sherman turns north and marches into South Carolina, burning the capital, Columbia, to the ground.
March 31– April 2, 1865	Grant breaks through at Petersburg and chases Lee's army into Virginia.
April 1865	Richmond, capital of the Confederacy, falls to Union forces. Lincoln enters the Confederate headquarters and sits in Jefferson Davis's chair.
	Lee surrenders to Grant at Appomattox. Lincoln is assassinated a few days later.
May 1865	End of hostilities with the surrender of General E. Kirby Smith at Shreveport, Louisiana.
April 1866	President Andrew Johnson declares the Civil War officially over.

FURTHER READING

Beller, Susan Provost. *To Hold This Ground: A Desperate Battle at Gettysburg.* New York: Margaret K. McElderry Books, 1995.

Carter, Alden R. *The Battle of Gettysburg.* New York: Franklin Watts, 1990.

Catton, Bruce. *The Battle of Gettysburg.* New York: American Heritage Books, 1963.

Damon, Duane. *When This Cruel War is Over: The Civil War Homefront.* Minneapolis, MN: Lerner, 1995.

Elish, Dan. *Harriet Tubman and the Underground Railroad.* Brookfield, CT: Millbrook Press, 1993.

Hughes, Christopher. *Battlefields Across America: Antietam.* Brookfield, CT: Twenty-First Century Books, 1998.

Johnson, Neil. *The Battle of Gettysburg.* New York: Four Winds, 1989.

Kerby, Mona. *Robert E. Lee: Southern Hero of the Civil War.* Springfield, NJ: Enslow Publishers, 1997.

McMullan, Kate. *The Story of Harriet Tubman, Conductor of the Underground Railroad.* Milwaukee: G. Stevens, 1997.

Marrin, Albert. *Virginia's General: Robert E. Lee and the Civil War.* New York: Atheneum, 1994.

Phillips, Charles. *My Brother's Face: Portraits of the Civil War in Photographs, Diaries, and Letters.* San Francisco: Chronicle, 1993.

Reef, Catherine. *Civil War Soldiers* (African-American Soldiers Series). New York: Twenty-First Century Books, 1993.

Steins, Richard. *Battlefields Across America: Shiloh.* New York: Twenty-First Century Books, 1997.

_____. *The Nations Divides: The Civil War (1820–1880).* New York: Twenty-First Century Books, 1993.

Tracey, Patrick Austin. *Military Leaders of the Civil War.* New York: Facts on File, 1993.

WEB SITES

There is a great deal of battle information, including the orders of battle for both sides and a description of each day's fighting, at the Battle of Gettysburg homepage:

http://www.mindspring.com/~murphy11/getty/

In addition, the Gettysburg Convention and Visitors Bureau provides a wealth of information including battle descriptions, area attractions, and battlefield maps at:

http://www.gettysburg.com

The National Park Service has its own Web site, part of which is devoted to Gettysburg National Military Park, at:

http://www.nps.gov/gett/index.htm

There is an international Civil War discussion group with a home page at:

http://www.arthes.com

> Among other things, this site maintains listings of the units and commanders involved in the battle of Gettysburg. For the Union, see:
>
> **http://www.arthes.com/gburg_un.html**
>
> For the Confederate commanders and units see:
>
> **http://www.arthes.com/gburg_co.html**

The Library of Congress also has an extensive Web site. One area is devoted to Lincoln's Gettysburg Address. It can be found at:

http://www.lcweb.loc.gov/exhibits/G.Address/ga.html

SOURCE NOTES

Part One

1. Quoted in James M. McPherson, *The Battle Cry of Freedom: The Civil War Era*, vol. 4 of *The Oxford History of the United States*, C. Vann Woodward, gen. ed. (New York: Oxford University Press, 1988), p. 82.

< 62 >

2. Ibid., p. 249.

Part Two

1. Quoted in Shelby Foote, *The Civil War: A Narrative*, vol. 2, *Fredericksburg to Meridian* (New York: Random House, 1963), pp. 445-446.

2. Ibid., p. 456.

3. Quoted in Bruce Catton, *The Army of the Potomac*, vol. 2, *Glory Road: The Bloody Route from Fredericksburg to Gettysburg* (New York: Doubleday and Company, 1952), p. 287.

4. Quoted in Foote, *The Civil War*, p. 464.

5. Quoted in Catton, *The Army of the Potomac*, vol. 1, *Mr. Lincoln's Army*, p. 286.

6. Quoted in Foote, *The Civil War*, p. 465.

7. Quoted in Edward J. Stackpole, *They Met at Gettysburg* (New York: Bonanza Books, 1956), p. 96.

8. Quoted in Champ Clark, *Gettysburg: The Confederate High Tide* (Alexandria, VA: Time-Life Books, 1985), p. 46.

9. Quoted in Albert A. Nofi, *The Gettysburg Campaign* (Conshohocken, PA: Combined Books, 1993), p. 67.

10. Quoted in James M. McPherson, ed., *The Atlas of the Civil War* (New York: Macmillan, Inc., 1994), p. 118.

11. Quoted in Glenn Tucker, *High Tide at Gettysburg* (Indianapolis, IN: Bobbs-Merrill Company, 1958), pp. 131-132.

12. Quoted in Clark, *Gettysburg*, p. 65.

13. Quoted in Tucker, *High Tide at Gettysburg*, p. 187.

14. Quoted in Geoffrey C. Ward, *The Civil War: An Illustrated History* (New York: Alfred A. Knopf, Inc., 1990), p. 218.

15. Ibid., p. 225.

16. Ibid.

< 63 >

17. Quoted in Patricia L. Faust, ed., *The Historical Times Illustrated Encyclopedia of the Civil War* (New York: Harper & Row, 1986), p. 498.

18. Quoted in James M. McPherson, *Gettysburg* (Atlanta, GA: Turner Publishing, 1993), p. 83.

19. Quoted in Robert Underwood Johnson and Clarence Clough Buel, eds., *The Tide Shifts*, vol. 3 of *Battles and Leaders of the Civil War*, (Secaucus, NJ: Castle, 1985), p. 343.

20. Quoted in Clark, *Gettysburg*, p. 134.

21. Quoted in Nofi, *The Gettysburg Campaign*, p. 185.

22. Quoted in George R. Stewart, *Pickett's Charge* (Boston: Houghton Mifflin, 1987), p. 199.

23. Ibid., p. 257.

24. Quoted in John W. Schildt, *Roads From Gettysburg* (Chewsville, MD: John W. Schildt, 1979), p. 23.

Part Three

1. Gary Wills, *Lincoln at Gettysburg* (New York: Simon & Schuster, 1992), 261.

OTHER SOURCES

Coddington, Edwin B. *The Gettysburg Campaign: A Study in Command.* New York: Charles Scribner's Sons, 1968.

Schlidt, John W. *Roads to Gettysburg.* Parsons, WV: McClain Printing, 1978.

Sufakis, Stewart. *Who was Who in the Civil War.* New York: Facts on File, 1988.

Taylor, Walter H. *Four Years with General Lee.* Bloomington, IN: Indiana University Press, 1962.

INDEX